SECRETS OF Magic

MIND-READING TRICKS

STEPHANIE TURNBULL

W
FRANKLIN WATTS
LONDON • SYDNEY

An Appleseed Editions book

First published in 2011 by Franklin Watts
338 Euston Road, London NW1 3BH

Franklin Watts Australia
Hachette Children's Books
Level 17/207 Kent St, Sydney, NSW 2000

© 2011 Appleseed Editions

Created by Appleseed Editions Ltd,
Well House, Friars Hill, Guestling,
East Sussex TN35 4ET

Designed and illustrated by Guy Callaby
Edited by Mary-Jane Wilkins
Picture research by Su Alexander

ISBN 978-1-4451-0370-9

Dewey Classification: 793.8

A CIP catalogue for this book is available from the British Library.

Picture credits:
l = left, r = right
Contents page l Eline Spek/Shutterstock, r Ljupco Smokovski; 4 Tomasz Trojanowski; 5 The Print
Collector/Alamy; 6 Paris Pierce/Alamy; 7 Geraint Lewis/Alamy; STILLFX/Shutterstock; 10 Bettmann/
Corbis; 12t Jocicalek/Shutterstock, b Shutterstock; 14 Getty Images; 15 The Protected Art Archive/Alamy;
16 Vikiri/Shutterstock; 17 Gio/Shutterstock; 18 Washington Post/Getty images; 23 Oote Boe Photography1/
Alamy; 24 RoxyFer/Shutterstock; 26 Bruno Passigatti/Shutterstock; 28 Kurhan/Shutterstock;
29 Mysterion the Mind Reader
Front cover: Kurhan/Shutterstock

Printed in Singapore

Franklin Watts is a division of Hachette Children's Books,
an Hachette UK company.
www.hachette.co.uk

Contents

Amazing Mind Power

IF YOU WANT to become a magician, then mind-reading tricks are the perfect way to astound your friends. This kind of magic is not too difficult to perform – and you can have fun pretending you know what people are thinking. Just remember the first rule of magic: never tell anyone how you did it!

TOP TIP
When performing, say 'tests' or 'experiments' instead of 'tricks'. It makes your magic sound more mysterious!

MENTALISM

Mind-reading tricks belong to a type of magic called mentalism, in which things seem to happen because of a magician's fantastic mental powers. Other mentalism effects include **telepathy** (see pages 24-25), fortune-telling and **hypnotism**, as well as tricks in which magicians appear to make things move or change using the power of their mind. Magicians who specialize in mentalism often call themselves mentalists.

*Some mentalists pretend to use the power of their mind to bend metal. They can create amazing effects with clever **sleight of hand** moves.*

FAKE PSYCHICS

In the past, many people used mentalism techniques to claim they had supernatural powers, for example to predict the future or contact the dead. They called themselves mediums, spiritualists or psychics, and used their skills to cheat people out of money. This was especially popular in Victorian times. Many magicians were angry that magic was used to cheat people, and revealed the methods used by mediums. Some magicians, such as James Randi (see below) still do this today.

This picture shows a Victorian medium attempting to contact the dead. Many mediums had hidden assistants who created spooky sound effects.

TRICK TYPES

Some mind-reading tricks are self-working, which means they rely on mathematical rules that always lead to the same outcome. Others use sneaky ways to make people pick a certain number, card or object. Many even use lying, faking and downright cheating! You can learn some of each type of trick in this book.

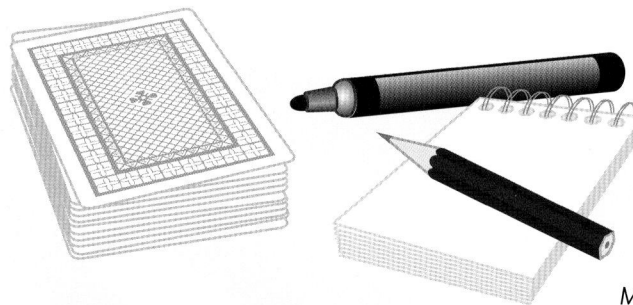

Most mind-reading magicians don't use elaborate props. This may be all you need.

MASTER MAGICIAN

JAMES RANDI (born 1928)

James Randi is a retired Canadian magician who performed many mentalism tricks. He also exposes fake psychics who use tricks to con people out of money. Since 1964, he has offered one million US dollars to anyone who can prove they have real psychic powers. No one has yet won the money. He famously appeared on a TV show with a man named James Hydrick, who claimed he could place a book on the table and turn pages using the power of his mind. As he was about to demonstrate this, Randi placed small pieces of polystyrene around the book. Hydrick was unable to perform his feat. Can you guess why? The answer is on page 32.

Tricks of the Trade

IN MIND-READING MAGIC, the way you perform tricks is extremely important. The magic must seem to come from the power of your mind, rather than from **props**, so you need to be confident and in control at all times. The secret is to practise until you can do your tricks perfectly, then work on your presentation style.

GREAT GUESSWORK

Mind-reading magicians need to be quick-thinking, and have a good memory. Many mentalists are successful because they mix magic tricks with other skills, such as making guesses about a person by studying their appearance, body language and other clues. This takes years of practice, but some magicians learn to do it so well that people are convinced they are psychic.

Magicians often pick up on obvious signs and make general statements that people can easily make fit their own personality.

This poster advertises Newmann the Great, who performed shows from the 1890s to the 1950s.

Magicians may also make vague guesses that mean different things to different people.

SMILEY FACE, SAD FACE

Here's a quick trick to get you started as a mentalist.

1. Tell the audience that you can sense what's drawn on a piece of paper without looking at it. Take a sheet of thin card or thick paper and draw nine faces, alternating smiley, sad, smiley, sad, in three rows of three.

2. Tear the paper into nine squares. Ask a volunteer to drop them into a bag and mix them up.

3. With your eyes closed, reach into the bag for a square. While you hold it in the bag, feel around the edges. The sad face squares all have one straight edge. The smiley face squares all have two straight edges, except for one that has no straight edges at all.

4. Announce "Smiley" or "Sad" every time you pull a square out of the bag. You'll be right every time! Afterwards, keep your audience guessing as to how you did it, saying, "Maybe I just got lucky each time... or did I?"

TOP TIP
Tricks like this are best done quickly, so you don't give people time to think about how they work. Remember to take away the squares afterwards so people can't study them!

MASTER MAGICIAN

DERREN BROWN (born 1971)

Derren Brown is an English mentalist who performs mind-reading on stage and television. He never claims to have real psychic powers – instead he combines tricks with lots of misdirection and showmanship. He is skilled at studying people so he can make good guesses about them, and he always picks volunteers who look as if they'll be easy to manipulate. He often pretends to reveal the secret of a trick, then follows it with something that can't be explained using that method. It's a good way of keeping his real methods secret, and leaves people more mystified than before!

PERFECT PATTER

One vital skill is using **patter** – in other words, what you say – to **misdirect** the audience's attention. For example, in the trick on the left, you need to keep talking while you're tearing the paper, so that people don't start to wonder why you aren't using scissors. You could also ask your volunteer to inspect the bag before putting the squares in it. This might fool them into thinking the bag must be the clue to the trick. Find more misdirection tips on pages 14 and 15.

Maths Magic

MATHEMATICAL TRICKS ARE designed to work every time, which makes them fairly easy to perform. You do need to remember exactly what to do, and in what order, otherwise they'll go wrong! This means practising them just as much as you practise other tricks.

You could give your volunteer a calculator when doing maths magic. You don't want them to get their sums wrong and ruin your trick!

THE MAGIC NUMBER

1. Ask a volunteer to write down any three-digit number, making sure that the first digit is higher than the last.

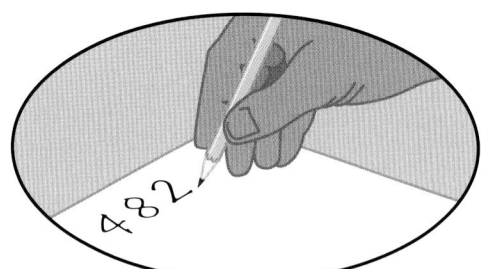

2. Now ask them to reverse the digits and write them again underneath, then subtract the second number from the first.

3. Ask them to reverse the digits of the total and write them underneath. Now ask them to add those two numbers. The answer will always be 1089.

4. Ask them to concentrate on the total while you read their mind. After pretending to study their face and think hard, write 1089 on a piece of paper and pass it to them. Ask if you're right. You will be!

DOUBLE DICE

1. While you turn your back, ask someone to throw two dice on the table.

2. Ask them to double the number of the first die, add five and then multiply by five.

$$2+2=4, \ 4+5=9, \ 9 \times 5=45$$

3. Now ask them to add the total to the number on the second die.

$$45+5=50$$

4. Ask them what their final figure is. In your head, subtract 25 from the answer they give and you'll get a two-digit number. The first digit is the first number thrown and the second is the other number thrown. Now pretend to concentrate on the dice and reveal the two numbers on them.

$$50-25=25$$

You threw a two... and a five!

Practise subtracting 25 from different figures so you'll be able to do it quickly.

PERSI DIACONIS

(born 1945)

Persi Diaconis is fascinated by two things: magic and maths. When he was 14, he ran away from home to tour with the American card magician Dai Vernon. Diaconis became a successful magician himself and studied the way that many magic tricks work using complicated mathematics. He even created new mathematical tricks of his own. When he was 24, Diaconis decided to devote himself to maths. He's now a mathematics professor.

TOP TIP
Remember that your audience doesn't know these are self-working tricks. Use your acting skills and present them with lots of drama.

MATHS OVERLOAD

If you're doing a mind-reading act, it's a good idea to use just one or two maths tricks and combine them with other mentalist magic – otherwise your audience might grow tired of sums! Try doing a maths trick as a short, one-off performance for your friends, during a lunch break. That way, you leave them wanting more!

Taking Risks

MIND-READING IS DIFFERENT from other types of magic because you can do tricks that take real risks – for example, offering a volunteer several choices, but relying on the fact that they will pick the most likely one. It's a technique that can go wrong – but if it works, it will amaze your audience.

Joseph Dunninger (see opposite)

NUMBER PICK

Here's an example of a simple but risky trick using probability.

1. Say to a friend, "Think of any number between 10 and 50. Make sure both digits are odd, and different from each other. Concentrate on that number."

In fact your friend won't have many numbers to choose from: 13, 15, 17, 19, 31, 35, 37 or 39. The funny thing is that most people choose 35 or 37.

2. Act as though you're reading their mind and write 35 on a piece of paper, then pretend to have second thoughts, cross it out and write 37.

3. Ask what their number was. If it was 37, reveal the paper and your correct prediction.

If it was 35, show them the paper and say, "The signals were a bit foggy... I should have gone with my first instinct!" Your friend will still be impressed.

If they choose a different number, just say that your mind-reading skills are rusty today... and move on to another trick. After all, it was a risk!

JOSEPH DUNNINGER (1892-1975)

Joseph Dunninger was known as *The Amazing Dunninger*. He was one of the most skilful mentalists ever. He performed on stage as well as on TV and radio, and even put on private shows for important people such as US presidents. He liked to sit on a stool with a pad of paper and a pencil, stunning audiences with his mind-reading abilities. Dunninger was an expert at using guesswork and probability in his act. It meant that he sometimes made mistakes, but he moved on from these so quickly that his audience only remembered the things he got right.

THE COMPLETE MIND-READING TEST

Here's a longer trick that combines maths and probability to give a really impressive result. It involves a lot of patter, which you must get exactly right.

Think of a number between one and ten.

Now multiply it by nine.

If the answer is two digits, add the two numbers together.

Take away five from the answer. Now think of the letter of the alphabet that corresponds to that number. One would be A, two would be B, and so on.

3

3 × 9 = 27

2 + 7 = 9

They don't know it, but this always leads to the number nine. Try it yourself and see!

9 - 5 = 4   4 = D

You know they'll end up with the letter D.

Now think of a country that begins with that letter.

Take the second letter of that country's name and pick an animal that begins with that letter.

Concentrate hard on the colour of that animal and I'll try to sense it. The colour I'm getting is… grey! Am I right?

Denmark

Elephant

This is where probability comes in. They could pick Denmark, the Dominican Republic, Djibouti or Dominica. Most people pick Denmark.

They could choose several animals, including an emu, earwig or echidna… but there's a more obvious choice!

TOP TIP
Keep the pace fast on this trick, so people go for the obvious choices and don't have time to think of obscure animals beginning with E!

Memory Magic

SOME MENTALISTS HAVE excellent memory skills. For example, they might memorize a long sequence of cards, then recall them so well that the audience is convinced there must be elaborate magic behind the trick. You don't need to train your memory to this extreme, but having a good memory helps with many mind-reading tricks.

*Memory experts can memorize huge chunks of books or telephone directories, or the order of a **deck** of cards.*

BRAIN TRAINING

The main way of storing lots of names, numbers or objects in your memory is to use a **mnemonic**. This involves turning random items into linked words or pictures that are easier to remember. For example, some people remember the colours of the rainbow (red, orange, yellow, green, blue, indigo and violet) by learning a sentence such as, 'Richard of York gave battle in vain', in which each initial letter represents a colour.

HARRY LORAYNE
(born 1926)

Harry Lorayne started training his memory at school to learn lists of facts and improve his grades. He went on to be a magician who performed all kinds of memory feats, such as reciting pages from phone books, or being introduced to hundreds of people then being able to name any of them at random. He has written books that explain how to use mnemonics to improve your memory.

Imagine you had to remember the words sun, train, door, owl, hat, cake and field. It might help to think of a scene something like this one.

CATCH THE KING

This trick was devised by Harry Lorayne (see left).
It's a self-working trick, but it takes memory skills to get it right.

1. Take out three queens and a king from a deck of cards. Ask a volunteer to stand next to you and lay the cards on the table in any order. Explain that you get such strong vibes from the king that you always know where it is without looking.

2. Tell the volunteer to swap the king with one of the cards next to it every time you shout, "Switch!" Demonstrate so they know what to do.

3. Remember the position of the king. Now turn away and ask someone to blindfold you so you can't see the cards.

4. Ask your volunteer to make a switch... then another... and more until they have made five switches in total.

Switch!... OK, do it again!...

5. Now pretend you're sensing where the king is. If the king was the first or third card, then it can't now be on the far left, so ask your volunteer to take the first card away. If the king was the second or fourth card, ask the person to remove the card on the far right instead.

He's still hiding from me... but I can tell he's not the first card on the left, so get rid of that one.

6. The king is now on the far left or right, but you can't know which. Ask the volunteer to make one more switch – which will bring the king into the middle.

Aha! I definitely felt him move that time!

7. Use your acting skills to pretend to sense where the king is. Tell the volunteer to remove the left hand card, then – after some hesitation – the right hand card. Of course they're left with the king!

I've got him! That's the king, isn't it?

TOP TIP
You can do this trick with all kinds of objects. You could 'sense' a £20 note among three £5 notes, or a bar of chocolate among three apples, or your mobile phone among three others. Use your imagination!

Fantastic Fakery

SOME MENTAL MAGIC involves faking your actions – in other words, saying you're doing one thing when doing something different. You'll need a lot of confidence and good acting skills, or your audience may become suspicious. Here's a trick in which you pretend to write one thing while writing another... plus performance tips to make it work.

The trick on this page involves a prediction in a sealed envelope. See page 27 for ideas on how to reveal this dramatically.

See page 27 for ideas on how to reveal this dramatically.

TOP TIP

Choose a subject that suits your audience – a pop star, TV personality, friend or teacher. Put a photo of the person in the envelope instead of writing their name. You could even choose different fruits and have the chosen one in a sealed box!

GUESS WHO?

Before you start, write on a piece of paper, "You will choose..." plus the name of a film star. Make sure it's someone your audience knows! Seal it in an envelope. You also need a notepad and pen, and a hat, box or bag to put pieces of paper in.

1. Place the hat on the table in front of you. Put the envelope next to it, saying there's a prediction in it.

2. Sit back with a notepad and ask people to call out names of film stars. When someone suggests a name, pretend to write it down, but instead write the name you put in the envelope. Tear off the sheet of paper, fold it up and put it in the hat.

Nicole Kidman

Brad Pitt

Nobody must see what you write!

3. Ask for more names, but write the same one each time. Stop when you have ten or more pieces of paper in the hat – and when someone has called out the name of the person in the envelope.

Brad Pitt

4. Now ask a volunteer to choose a piece of paper from the hat and read out the name.

5. Emphasize that there's no way you could know which name they'd pick. Now ask them to open the envelope and see your prediction!

You will choose Brad Pitt

MISDIRECTION MOVES

For this trick to work, you need to misdirect the audience. Keep talking and looking up as you write so that people don't focus too hard on the pen and paper. Make comments about the person whose name you're supposed to be writing to get other people talking too. If it's a long or difficult name, ask someone to spell it and pretend to write the letters they say. You could write one name they suggest, but pretend to make such a mess that you throw aside that piece of paper and start again – making sure the audience sees the discarded paper and the name on it.

LOOK AT ME!

Another good misdirection method is to use someone's name when you talk to them. It's more personal, so it's more likely to make someone look at you and listen to what you're saying. Look them in the eye while talking, as this forces them to look back.

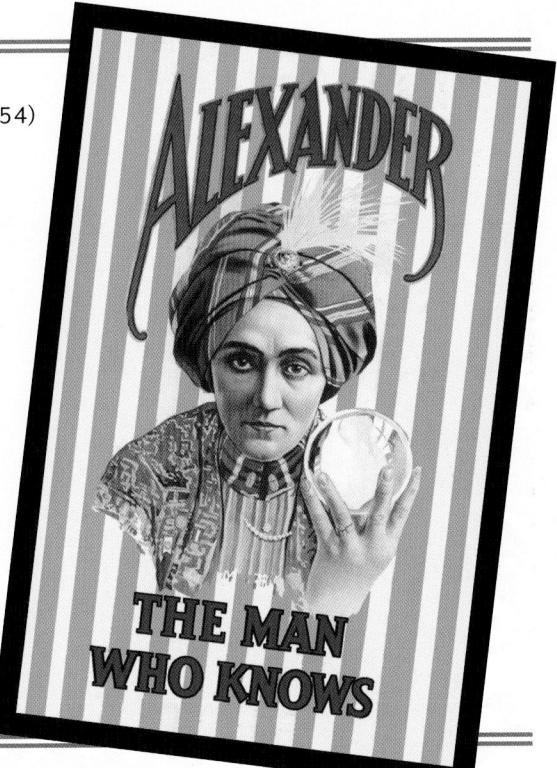

ALEXANDER (1880-1954)

Alexander was one of the most successful mentalists ever. He called himself Alexander, The Man Who Knows, and performed mind-reading, fortune-telling and telepathy tricks to huge audiences in the 1920s. He had an exciting performance style, which entertained his audience, but also helped misdirect their attention. For example, he dressed in long, sweeping robes, wore a large feathered turban on his head and often used a crystal ball. Audiences were mesmerized by his acting skills and fooled by his tricks. Cheating came naturally to him – he was also a **con man** who went to prison several times.

Brilliant Book Tests

IF YOU WANT to be a mind-reading magician, it's important to know a book test. These are classic mind-reading tricks in which someone memorizes a word from a book and you then appear to read their mind and announce the word. There are many different ones, some more complicated than others. Here are two to try.

You can use any type of book for book tests – novels, textbooks or even dictionaries.

GOOD WITH WORDS

For this trick, you need a few books of similar thickness.

1. Ask a volunteer to choose a book. Pick it up and flick through it as you explain that you're going to ask them to focus on a word, which you will then predict. Near the middle, secretly – and quickly – memorize a page number and the first word on the page.

smiled

Remember these two things!

99

2. Hand the book to the volunteer and ask them to choose another book. Take the second book and start to flick through it, asking the volunteer to tell you when to stop. Try to make sure you're somewhere near the middle when they do.

Stop!

You stopped me at page 99

3. Pretend to look at and say the page number, but in fact say the number you memorized. Shut the book again straight away.

85

4. Now ask the volunteer to look at that page in their book and concentrate hard on the first word on the page. After pretending to think hard, announce the word you memorized.

smiled

I'm getting a happy word... smiled!

Ace Marks the Place

For this book test, you need a thick book with plain covers. Try taking the cover off an old hardback. You also need two ace of hearts playing cards from identical decks.

She ran home as fast as she could.

1. Before you start, memorize the first sentence from a left hand page somewhere near the middle of the book. Put a playing card face up in the book to mark the page. Make sure it sticks out a bit.

2. Begin by showing your audience the closed book, with the card facing you so they can't see it. Give a volunteer the second card, face up, and ask them to put it in the book near the middle.

3. Turn away to pick up a pen and notepad. As you move, turn the book round and push the volunteer's card into the book so it can't be seen. Use patter to direct the audience's attention away from the book and towards the pad and paper.

4. Pass the book to your volunteer with your card sticking out towards them. Ask them to open it at the marked page and memorize the first full sentence on the left side. Of course, this is the one you memorized! Pretend to read their mind, scribble the sentence on the pad... then reveal it.

She ran home as fast as she could.

An artistic twist

An alternative to writing is to draw. For example, in the Ace Marks the Place trick, ask your volunteer to concentrate on their sentence. You can then sketch the impressions you claim to be receiving from them. You choose the page, so you can pick a paragraph you like and decide beforehand what you're going to draw!

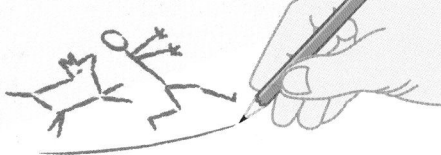

MASTER MAGICIAN

RICHARD OSTERLIND

(born 1948)

Richard Osterlind is an American mentalist who has created many mind-reading effects and routines that are often used by other magicians. Like every good mind-reading magician, he has his own amazing book trick. In his version, an audience member picks a word from a newspaper, which Osterlind then predicts. Although his method is secret, you can bet that he somehow forces the person to pick a certain word!

Forcing a Choice

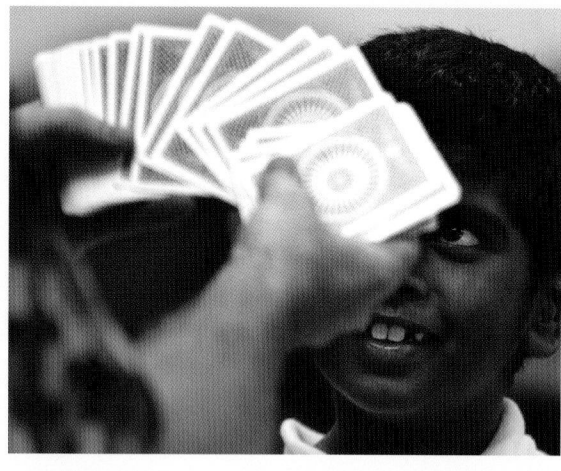

Many card tricks begin with a magician forcing a volunteer to pick a certain card. The volunteer thinks the magic is yet to come, when the magician has already done their sneaky moves!

AS YOU'VE SEEN, many tricks work because the magician already knows which card or object a volunteer will pick – so it's easy to 'read their mind' and guess it! Making a volunteer choose a certain thing (while they think they have a free choice) is called a force. Here are a few useful forces.

CLASSIC CARD FORCES

Many mind-reading card tricks force a volunteer to pick a card you know. One way to do this is to glimpse the bottom card as you pick up the deck.

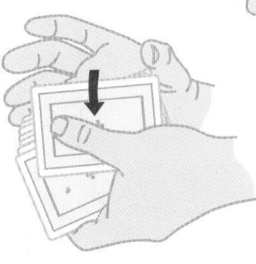

Next, move the bottom card to the top. You do this by shuffling the cards. Hold them in your hand as shown, then lift most of the deck and drop a few cards on either side of the cards in your hand. Make sure you drop the last card, on its own, on top of the deck.

Now you can offer the top card to your volunteer, knowing what it is.

THE MAGICIAN'S CHOICE

The Magician's Choice is useful when you want to make a volunteer narrow down several objects to one particular item, while making them feel that they are making their own choices. Here's what you do.

Let's say you have two books, red and blue. You want your volunteer to pick the red one. Ask them to point to a book.

If it's the red one, then say, "OK, you've chosen the red book" and hand it over.

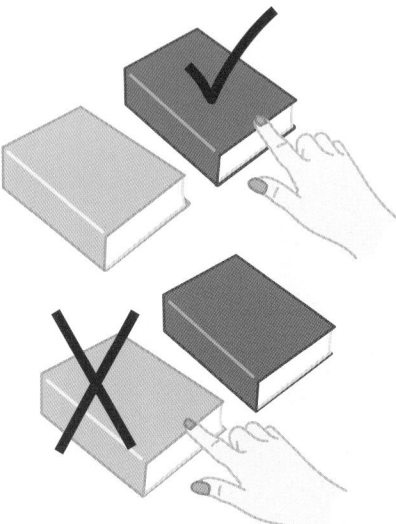

If they point to the blue book, say, "OK, we'll get rid of that one," and move it aside, leaving them with the red book.

You can do this with three books. First, ask the volunteer to point to two. Keep them if the chosen book is one of them, and discard them if not. If you're left with the chosen book, then you're done. If you're left with two books, go through the steps above.

THE ELIMINATION GAME

You need nine objects for this trick – for example, nine CDs, photos, cards or toys. Decide beforehand which one you want your volunteer to pick. Write its name on a piece of paper, then seal this in an envelope.

You will be left with the fire engine

1. Put the envelope on the table and spread out the objects. Explain that you and a volunteer will remove objects, one by one, until there's only one left. To make it fair, you'll take turns: you'll choose two things and they will decide which one to get rid of, then they will choose two things and you'll take one away.

I'll start by picking these two... and you remove one.

2

So we did that fairly, right? The only problem is, you're playing this game with a mind-reader...

4

2. Start by selecting two items. Don't pick your chosen item. Ask your volunteer to remove one of them from the table.

3. Now it's the volunteer's turn. If one of their choices is your chosen item, remove the other one. If neither is your chosen item, then it doesn't matter which you remove.

4. Take turns until there are two objects left on the table. One will be yours. It's also your turn to remove one object – so you can't lose! Remove the other object.

5. Now ask the volunteer to open the envelope, revealing your correct prediction.

TOP TIP
You can play with more than nine objects. Just remember that if there is an odd number of items, you pick first. If there is an even number, your volunteer picks first. That way, you'll always be the one making the final choice.

One Step Ahead

MANY MIND-READING TRICKS rely on a volunteer choosing something you've forced on them. In other tricks, you can let someone have a free choice – and you'll still know what they chose! The secret is the one-ahead principle. You need to know one piece of information before you start, and use this to stay a move ahead of the audience. Try these tricks to see how it works.

CARD-SENSING HANDS

1. Take a deck of cards and ask a volunteer to shuffle them. Tell the audience you can identify cards by moving your hands over them... and that you can pass on the skill to a volunteer! As you talk, take the deck and glimpse the bottom card.

2. Now you need to spread the cards across the table. First, fan the deck out like this – and put your little finger on the bottom card.

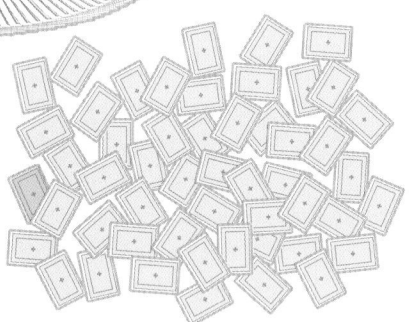

3. Slide the cards around with your hands, keeping your finger on the bottom card. Make sure your card ends up near the edge, and remember its position.

Now try to sense a card... let's say the two of spades. Touch it when you think you've found it.

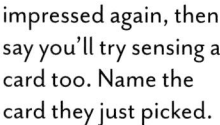

4. Ask a volunteer to hold their hands over the cards, and pretend to transmit your card-sensing powers to them. Now ask them to sense a card – and name the one you know.

That's very good... OK, let's go for a picture card – say the jack of hearts.

5. Pick up the card they choose, look at it then set it aside. Look impressed, as if they really did pick the two of spades. Now ask them to try to sense another card – and this time name the card they picked.

6. Again, pick up and look at the card they choose. Pretend to be impressed again, then say you'll try sensing a card too. Name the card they just picked.

7. Pretend to sense the card... and pick up the card you knew from the start of the trick. Look at it and smile, as if you were right.

8. Now pick up all three chosen cards, slipping the third one underneath. Remind the audience which cards you were trying to sense – then reveal them one by one.

So we tried to find the two of spades, the jack of hearts and the three of diamonds... and guess what, we did!

I KNOW ALL ABOUT YOU!

This one-ahead trick works well with a group of friends. Prepare several days ahead by sneakily finding out something about a friend that they wouldn't expect you to know. Let's say you discover that their first pet was called Fluffy.

Think of the name of your favourite teacher at primary school.

1. Tell the friend you're going to ask them three personal questions. Ask a question and pretend to read their mind for the answer. Write Fluffy on a piece of paper, fold it and put it on the table.

Fluffy

2. Now ask them to say – for the benefit of the audience – the name they were thinking of.

Mrs Ward

3. Ask a second question. Pretend to read their mind again and write their first answer on another piece of paper. Fold it and place it on top of the first.

Where would you most like to go on holiday?

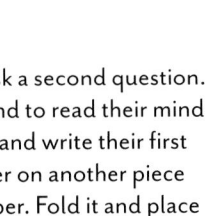

Mrs Ward

4. Again, ask your friend to tell the audience what they were thinking of.

Peru

5. Finally, ask the question that gives you the answer you knew before starting the trick. Write down your friend's second answer, fold the paper and put it on the pile.

What was the name of your first pet?

Peru

6. As before, ask them the name they were thinking of.

Fluffy

7. Now pick up the slips and unfold them one by one to reveal the correct answers. Pull out the middle slip first, otherwise your predictions will be in the wrong order!

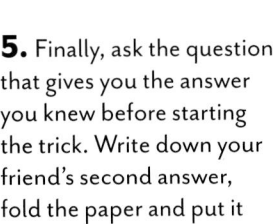

Fluffy

Peru

Mrs Ward

TOP TIP

Don't forget to listen carefully to the answers your volunteer gives! You'll need to remember them for a while before you write them down.

Secret Helpers

MAGICIANS DON'T ALWAYS work alone. Sometimes they have a secret helper in the audience who passes on information, letting the magician perform mind-reading feats. If you work with a friend like this, you must create a code and practise it until you both know what you're doing. You also need to make your friend promise never to reveal the secret!

THE TELLTALE CHAIR

This trick is best performed for a small group of friends at a party. One must be your secret assistant. You need a line of five chairs.

1. Beforehand, you and your friend think of a code word for each chair.

I   You   It   We   They

2. At the party, line up the chairs and explain that your mental powers are so strong that you can sense which chair has been used. Ask a friend to choose a chair and sit on it for a few seconds while you're out of the room. Choose a volunteer – your secret helper – to guard the door while you're outside.

3. When someone has sat on a chair and got up again, your helper calls you, making sure their first word is the code word of the chair that was used. For example, for the first chair they could say, "I think you can come in now," for the second they could say, "You can come in now," and so on.

We're ready for you now!

4. Pretend to sense 'vibes' from each chair before announcing which is the chosen one.

TOP TIP
You could create another code to identify each friend, so you could also 'sense' who sat in the chair. For example, if the person is called Abby Taylor, your helper could say, "Amazing trick!"

SILENT CODES

Your secret helper can also give you information silently using hand or body positions. You could put a card on a table and leave the room, saying that someone should pick up the card and sit on it while you're out. When you come back, your helper can indicate who took the card. Try these methods – or make up your own.

Sometimes magicians have secret assistants sitting in the audience, ready to help with tricks. These helpers are often known as stooges.

Your helper sits with legs crossed and points a foot in the direction of the person with the card.

The helper uses fingers to indicate the chair the person is sitting in.

The helper sits in the same position as the person with the card.

Telepathy Tricks

IF YOU WANT to perform with a friend, try creating a telepathy act, in which you seem to communicate using only thoughts. Telepathy routines rely on codes, as do secret helper tricks. These tricks will make your friend appear as magical as you... so only do them if you don't mind sharing the spotlight!

It makes sense to perform with your best friend or a close family member, so it seems possible that you really could be telepathic!

DARING DOUBLE ACTS

During a telepathy act a magician usually walks through the audience and takes items people offer. They then ask their assistant – who is on stage, perhaps blindfolded – to name the item, using code words that tell the assistant what it is. Codes usually use common words to represent certain letters or words. The more complicated you make your code, the harder it is for the audience to detect.

SILENT TELEPATHY

Instead of using a code, you and your friend could memorize a list of items that audience members are likely to give you during the act. See page 12 for ideas on how to memorize lists.

Ask the audience to hold up items to be identified. Try to choose items in the order you memorized them. Each time, say, "What am I holding now?"

As with all memory stunts, it's a little risky, but if it works well people won't have a clue how you did it!

Right, please guess now!

right = red, please = p, guess = e, now = n

I'm sensing a pen... a red one!

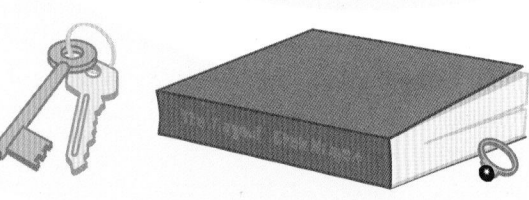

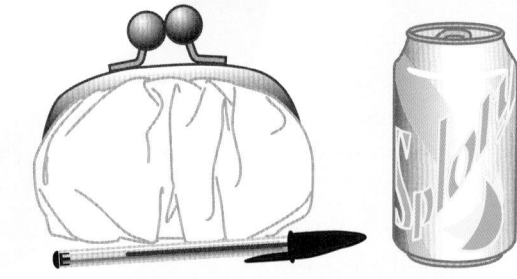

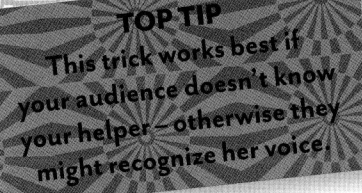

TOP TIP
This trick works best if your audience doesn't know your helper – otherwise they might recognize her voice.

TELEPATHIC TELEPHONE FRIEND

Here's a great telepathy trick to perform at a party.

1. Before the party, you and your helper need to make a code name for each card in a deck. If your helper is female, these must be girls' names. If your helper is male, use boys' names. The last letter, sound or consonant of the first name should reveal the card's suit, for example:

Sarah = Hearts   Jade = Diamonds
Jackie = Clubs   Alice = Spades

The first letter of the surname corresponds to the card's number, for example:

Ace (1) = Anderson   8 = Henderson
2 = Bull   9 = Irving
3 = Carter   10 = Jones
4 = Daniels   Jack (11) = Keith
5 = Emerson   Queen (12) = Lewis
6 = Franks   King (13) = Matthews
7 = Grant

Practise with a deck of cards until you can say the 'name' of each card without hesitating.

2. When you perform this trick, make sure your helper is at home near their phone. Ask a volunteer to name any card. Now think of the name that corresponds to that card.

3. Tell the audience you have a friend, in this case Jade, and that the two of you are telepathic. Offer to prove it by transmitting the name of the card to Jade using thought waves. Now give the volunteer your helper's number and ask them to dial it. Tell them to ask for Jade Lewis, then ask her to guess the card.

Queen of diamonds   Jade Lewis

Hello, is that Jade Lewis?

Yes

4. As soon as your helper hears the code name, she can say what the card was... without a word from you!

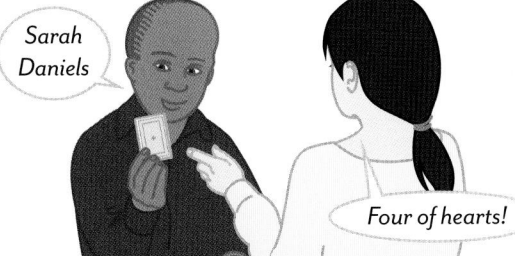

Sarah Daniels

Four of hearts!

Marlo the Magnificent is thinking of a card. Do you know what it is?

I'm getting a red card... with a picture... it's the queen of diamonds!

MASTER MAGICIAN

AGNES (1850-1916) AND JULIUS ZANCIG (1857-1929)

Julius and Agnes Zancig were a Danish couple who performed a telepathy act. Their code was so complex that they must have practised for hours every day to learn, extend and refine it. Even other magicians couldn't figure it out. It's still a mystery today. The Zancigs were also successful because they combined their code with magic tricks. For example, a reporter once handed Julius a sealed envelope and challenged Agnes to predict the word written on a card inside. Sure enough, she managed it, even though Julius never opened the envelope. Can you guess how? Find the answer on page 32.

Surprise Endings

MENTALISM ACTS WORK best when the magician keeps surprising the audience with different, unusual methods of ending tricks. You can do this too – it just takes planning and plenty of imagination. Here are a few ideas to get you started. They're fun to do and will all add to the general spookiness of your act!

The moment when you reveal a person's card or your prediction needs to be jaw-dropping. Don't rush it! Pause to create tension, then make the revelation slow and dramatic.

SILLY SCIENCE

A great way to baffle your audience is to pretend you're using a scientific method. Let's say you've forced a card on a volunteer. Now spread out the cards and announce that you will find the chosen one using the person's body language – for example, their movements. Make up whatever you want.

Pretend the person's body language is leading you towards the card. Hold up a few nearby cards and look closely at the person each time. Now hold up the chosen one. Of course your volunteer will be trying really hard to keep perfectly still.

Smile, as if you spotted something in their face. Say, "It's this one, isn't it?" The person will spend the rest of the day wondering how they gave it away!

GREAT GIMMICKS

How about making your prediction appear out of thin air? To do this, slip to the bathroom before the trick and write the prediction on your arm with a small piece of soap. For example, if you plan to force the two of hearts card on a volunteer, draw a number two and a heart. Then, when it's time to reveal your prediction, roll up your sleeve and shake pepper on your arm. Gently rub it in, so it sticks to the soap. Blow off the loose pepper to reveal the correct answer.

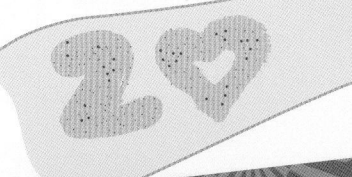

I NEVER TOUCHED IT!

If your prediction is in an envelope, keep the envelope well away from you throughout. Instead of putting it on the table, ask a volunteer to hold it or put it in their pocket. When they open the envelope, they'll be more impressed.

HIDE AND SEEK

Another method is to hide the envelope beforehand – for example, under the volunteer's seat cushion. When you're ready to reveal the prediction, ask the person to look under the cushion and find the envelope! Use your imagination to think of other good hiding places.

TOP TIP
When writing with soap on your arm, keep things simple. A couple of big, clear letters or shapes show up best.

MASTER MAGICIAN

MAX MAVEN (born 1950)

Max Maven performs mentalism tricks on stage and appears on TV shows all over the world. He works hard to keep his audiences on the edge of their seats by creating inventive and surprising routines. Other magicians often employ him to liven up their acts with exciting performance ideas. He claims to read more than 150 books and magazines a month, which give him ideas for new and unusual mind-reading effects.

You will choose the Two of Hearts

Your prediction could appear anywhere!

Show Time!

YOU'VE PRACTISED THE mind-reading tricks in this book until you can do them in your sleep. You've perfected brilliant endings that will stun your audience. You've worked out great patter to go with each trick. Now it's time to put it all together and stage a show! Here are some ideas to make sure your act is a success.

LOOK THE PART

The way you look on stage affects how the audience responds. Some mentalists try to look mysterious and spooky, with dramatic dyed hair, strange clothes and makeup to emphasize their eyes. Others prefer to look smart and professional. Whichever image you choose, make sure you appear cool, commanding and confident. You'll be giving people orders and you need them to do as you say.

Think of yourself as an actor and put all your energy into playing the role. If you feel awkward or embarrassed, the audience will too.

SPECIAL EFFECTS

Try using scenery and lighting to create an eerie mood on stage. You could dim the lights to make looming shadows, or use coloured bulbs to give your skin a strange glow! Creating the right atmosphere helps put your audience in the mood for mysterious magic. The more they enjoy themselves, the more they'll believe that you have genuine powers!

FUNNY STUFF

Most mentalists prefer to be serious, as jokes or **slapstick** humour might ruin the mood. Don't be too serious though – you're entertaining people, not lecturing them. You can make a few funny comments to break the tension, or to misdirect attention, but never be rude, or you'll turn your audience against you.

I need you to clear you mind... Wow, that was quick!

A few jokes can help relax your audience!

WHEN DISASTER STRIKES...

Even great mentalists make mistakes from time to time, especially when they rely on guesswork or memory. If a trick goes wrong, distract people by saying, "I'm getting a lot of interference with my thought waves today. I think somebody left their mobile on..." The chances are that someone did – so you might end up turning the mistake into another example of your amazing mental powers! Then move on quickly to the next trick.

MASTER MAGICIAN

MYSTERION THE MIND-READER (born 1974)

Mysterion the Mind-Reader is a Canadian mentalist who dresses in black and has a white streak in his hair that makes him look striking on stage. He also has an exciting stage act, filled with spooky characters such as his sidekick, Wolfman, as well as circus-style stunts and live music. His shows are a big success because they're so entertaining, and he's careful to make his sinister style so exaggerated that it's funny rather than scary!

Glossary

con man
Short for confidence man; someone who appears to be honest but in fact cheats people out of money.

deck
Another word for a pack or full set of playing cards.

force
A way of seeming to offer a volunteer a random choice of cards or other items, when in fact you are making sure they pick the one you want them to have.

hypnotism
The act of putting someone into a kind of trance, in which they feel relaxed, but also awake and alert. If someone is hypnotized by a magician, they can often be persuaded to alter their behaviour or thoughts. Hypnotism is also used to help people change unhealthy habits, such as smoking.

misdirect
To draw an audience's attention away from something you don't want them to see or think too much about.

mnemonic
A rhyme, word, phrase, picture or anything else that helps you to remember something important.

patter
Prepared, practised speech that magicians use when performing magic tricks. Although you need to work out your patter beforehand, make sure you speak naturally and don't read it out like a script.

probability
A measure of how likely it is that something will happen, taking into account all the possible outcomes.

prop
Short for property; any object that is used to help perform a trick.

slapstick
Silly, funny and over-the-top. Clowns often perform slapstick comedy, for example chasing around or pretending to slip on banana skins.

sleight of hand
The technique of secretly moving, altering or swapping objects to create a magical effect. Sleights (pronounced 'slights') take a lot of practice to perform well, and also rely on good misdirection skills.

telepathy
The ability to share thoughts or feelings with someone else without using words or any other physical methods of communication.

Websites

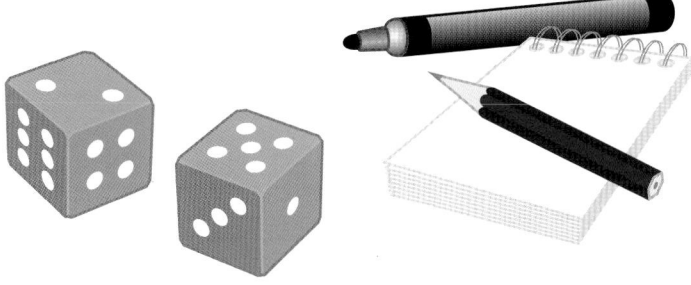

www.magictricks.com/library
Read biographies of famous magicians and discover fascinating facts about their lives and the tricks they invented.

www.freemagictricks4u.com/free-mentalism.html#VisitorPages
Check out lots of mentalism tricks contributed by amateur magicians.

http://faculty.washington.edu/chudler/chmemory.html
Start training your memory by playing all kinds of memory games, then try out different methods for memorizing things.

www.geniimagazine.com/wiki/index.php/Main_Page
Discover hundreds of articles about famous magicians and clever trick techniques, all written by magic enthusiasts. Go to the Mentalism page to find out about classic mind-reading routines.

www.themagiccircle.co.uk
Find out about the Magic Circle, an old and famous magic society that only the best magicians in the world are allowed to join – after they've passed a strict interview, performance exam and vote!

www.theyoungmagiciansclub.com
Learn about the Young Magician's Club, a group set up by the Magic Circle and open to all 10-18 year olds who are interested in magic. There is a fee to join, but members then receive newsletters, magazines, free tricks and advice from a panel of magic experts.

Index

SECRETS OF MAGIC... REVEALED!

Page 5 Why couldn't James Hydrick turn the pages?

Answer: *James Hydrick usually performed his feat by secretly blowing on the pages. He couldn't do this with the polystyrene pieces in place, as they would have moved and exposed the method behind the trick.*

Page 25 How did Julius Zancig see inside the sealed envelope?

Answer: *For this trick, Julius Zancig used pure alcohol, which can be dabbed on to paper to make it see-through. It soon dries and the paper returns to normal. Julius had a small sponge soaked in alcohol, which he hid in his armpit. When the reporter handed Julius the envelope, he casually held it under his arm, letting the alcohol soak in and turn the envelope transparent. It was then easy for him to see the word on the card and communicate this to Agnes in code. By the time he returned the envelope to the reporter, it had dried.*